The Original

BIGFOOT

ABC

Alphabet Book

R.D. Warner

ISBN: 9798374007770 (paperback)

Library of Congress Control Number: 2023901081

First Edition, 2023.

Author: R.D. Warner

Artwork: R.D. Warner, utilizing DALL·E 2 A.I.

Design and Layout: R.D. Warner

Publisher: R.D. Warner—Maple Valley, WA, USA

Printer: Kindle Direct Publishing; in the United States of America.

Image credit (Composite satellite photograph of North America, Page "O"): CC0 1.0 Universal (CC0 1.0) Public Domain Ded[ica]tion. Original public domain image from Wikimedia Commons.

<u>**Author Contact:**</u> **RDWarner.Creative@gmail.com / www.BigfootABC.com**

---

www.BigfootABC.com

While supplies last, all artwork in this book is available for purchase in large scale LIMITED EDITION print form[s.] Purchase and licensing information is available on our website.

For Allison, Elena, Preston, Chewy, Tito, Smoky, Spicy, Carl and Kona (and Bigfoot).

The **ABOMINABLE** Snowman lives in the Himalayas, which is **A** really tall mountain range in **ASIA**. He is **A** large **APELIKE ANIMAL** with fuzzy white fur.

BIGFOOT is **BIPEDAL**. That means he walks on 2 feet. He also has a **BIG BUTT**.

BIGFOOT got **BACK**!

Until Bigfoot is officially discovered by scientists, he will **CONTINUE** to be **CLASSIFIED** as a **CRYPTID**. That means he is a **CREATURE** that has not been proven to exist (yet).

DISCOVERING Bigfoot would be a really big **DEAL**. Unfortunately, he may never **DECIDE** to **DIVULGE** himself. He is a master of **DISGUISE**, and can easily **DISAPPEAR** into the **DENSE DARK** forest.

Ee

Bigfoot is **ELUSIVE** and **EVASIVE**. That means he is very hard to catch. People also say Bigfoot is **ENIGMATIC** because his **EXISTENCE** is so mysterious.

Bigfoot has big **FEET**, and he leaves big **FOOTPRINTS** in the **FOREST**. That's why we call him Bigfoot.

Some people think Bigfoot is a long-lost relative of **GIGANTOPITHECUS**, a **GARGANTUAN** ape that went extinct more than 100,000 years ago.

Bigfoot might be an undiscovered **HOMINID**. That means **HE** could be related to orangutans, gorillas, chimpanzees, and even **HUMANS**.

Bigfoot **IS INTELLIGENT** and he lives **IN ISOLATION**. That's why he's so hard to find.

Jj
When Bigfoot is young, he is called a JUVENILE. JUST like human children, he likes to JUMP and run through the forest.

Bigfoot **KNOCKS** on trees with big sticks. He doesn't have a telephone, so this is how he calls his friends.

Bigfoot is a **LARGE** hairy creature. People say he can grow to be over 10 feet tall and weigh up to 2,000 pounds.

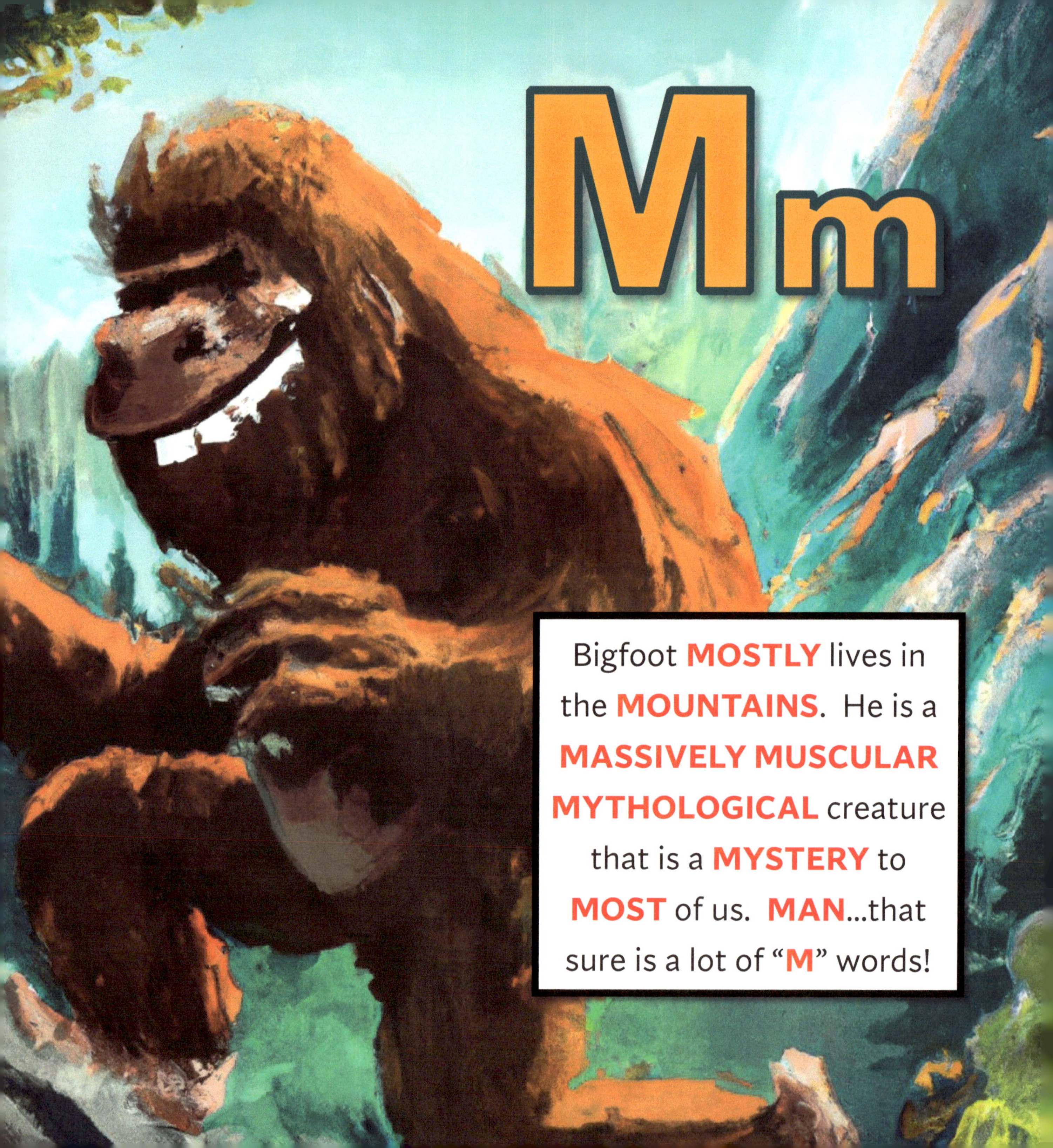

Bigfoot **MOSTLY** lives in the **MOUNTAINS**. He is a **MASSIVELY MUSCULAR MYTHOLOGICAL** creature that is a **MYSTERY** to **MOST** of us. **MAN**...that sure is a lot of "**M**" words!

Nn

Bigfoot may be a **NONHUMAN** primate, just like monkeys and apes.

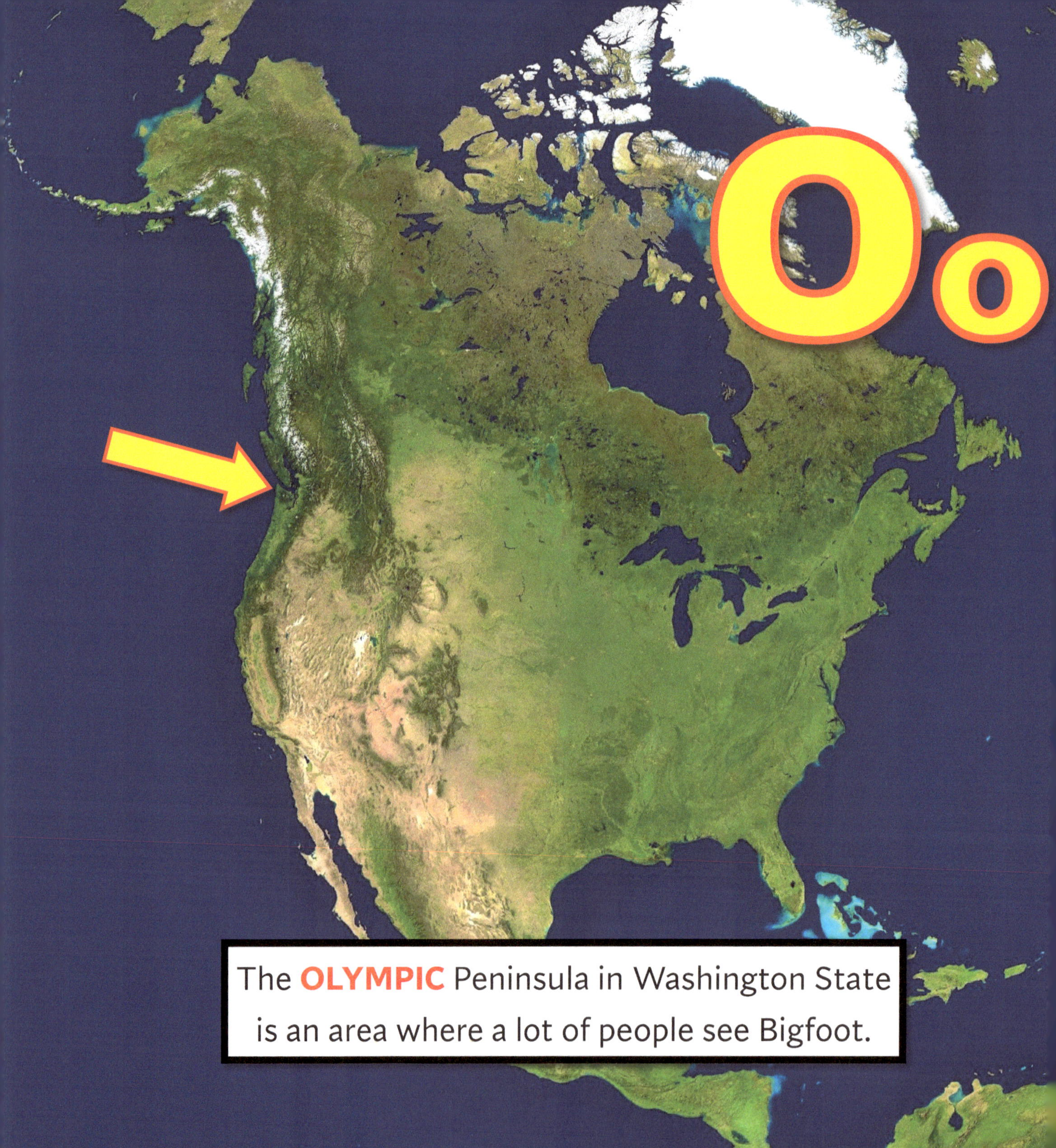

The **OLYMPIC** Peninsula in Washington State is an area where a lot of people see Bigfoot.

The **PATTERSON-GIMLIN** film is the most famous **PROOF** of Bigfoot's existence. It was recorded in 1967 near Bluff Creek in Northern California. Some **PEOPLE** suspect it was a hoax. However, no one has ever **PROVEN** that it's **PHONY**.

Until Bigfoot is proven to exist, people will always **QUESTION** if he is real. What do you think?

Rr
Bigfoot likes to throw ROCKS at people. This is a RARE occurrence. If it ever happens to you...RUN!

Bigfoot is **SOMETIMES** called **SASQUATCH**. People also call him the **SKUNK** Ape because he is **SERIOUSLY STINKY**!

Bigfoot builds **TREMENDOUSLY TALL TREE**-structures in **THE** woods **THAT** look like **TRANSPARENT TIPIS**. No one knows why, but I **THINK THEY** are **TOTALLY TERRIFIC**.

Bigfoot is an **UNDISCOVERED** species that is **UNKNOWN** to science. To prove he exists, **UNDENIABLE** evidence will be required. I wonder if he was brought here by a **UFO**.

Bigfoot is known for his **VERY** loud **VOCALIZATIONS**. That means he **VIGOROUSLY** uses his **VOICE** to whoop and whistle in **VARIOUS** ways.

A long **WHILE** ago, people called Bigfoot the **WILD-MAN**. In some parts of the **WORLD**, he is called the **WOOD** Booger. I **WONDER** if a **WITNESS** has ever **WATCHED** him pick his nose **WITH** a stick (ew!)

Bigfoot may suffer from **XENOPHOBIA**. That means he might have an irrational fear of strangers, or dislike people just because they don't live in the forest.

YETI is what people call Bigfoot in the Himalayas.
He is called the **YOWIE** in Australia.

Zz
If Bigfoot is ever discovered, I hope they don't put him in a ZOO. He needs to live in the forest with his friends and family.
Do you agree?

Dedicated to Wes Germer, host of Sasquatch Chronicles.
Without your show, this book would never exist. I've spent way too many hours listening.

For those unfamiliar with the Sasquatch Chronicles podcast, you need to check it ou

Curt, I'm also dedicating this to you. Thanks for turning me on to Sasquatch Chronicles.